G

TIGER BOOKS INTERNATIONAL

past and present

CASTLES OF BAVARIA

Text
Paola Calore

Graphic design
Anna Galliani

Editing Supervision
Ombretta Finotello

Translation
A.B.A., Milan

Art Director
Patrizia Balocco Lovisetti

1 The picture shows a detail of the frescoes covering the walls of the Singers' Room, in Neuschwanstein castle. The peacock was one of Ludwig II's favourite emblems; the hidden symbolism may be that despite its magnificent appearance, the peacock cannot lift its wings in flight, and like the king must remain bound to the reality of the material world.

2/7 Johannisburg Castle is one of the most important works of the German Renaissance and provides a magnificent introduction to the architecture of state castles typical of the modern era.

3-6 Ludwig II of Bavaria's last dream was Herrenchiemsee Castle. The hundreds of candles used to illuminate it were lighted when the king was in the castle; he loved to wander about admiring his image reflected in the mirrors by the flickering, eerie candlelight.

This edition published in 1998 by TIGER BOOKS INTERNATIONAL PLC , 26a York Street Twickenham TW1 3LJ, England.

First published by Edizioni White Star.
Title of the original edition:
Castelli della Baviera.
© World copyright 1998 by Edizioni White Star,
Via Candido Sassone 22/24, 13100
Vercelli, Italy.

ISBN 1-84056-019-3

Printed in Italy by Grafedit, Bergamo (Italy).
Colour separations by Mazzucchelli, Milan (Italy).

CONTENTS

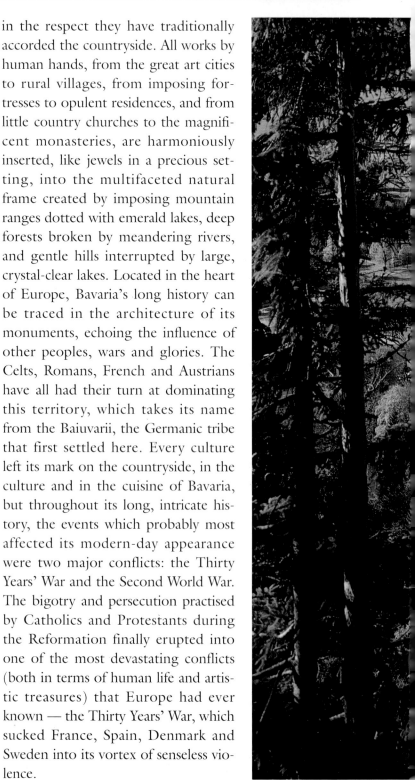

*B*avaria's unconventional status within the Federal Republic of Germany is confirmed by the title that this Land, the largest and oldest of the sixteen *Länder* of Germany, uses when it proclaims its boundaries in official documents and signs: *Freistaat Bayern* (the Free State of Bavaria). In all of Germany, no one is as proud of their own uniqueness and independence as the Bavarians, a romantic and combative people that forged the history of Europe for centuries. Bavarians often express their loyalty in descending order: "First Bavaria, then Europe, and then Germany," and in fact they have every right to be proud of their land. Essentially, the only thing missing in its endless list of natural beauties is the sea. The great love that Bavarians have always had for their land can be seen in the respect they have traditionally accorded the countryside. All works by human hands, from the great art cities to rural villages, from imposing fortresses to opulent residences, and from little country churches to the magnificent monasteries, are harmoniously inserted, like jewels in a precious setting, into the multifaceted natural frame created by imposing mountain ranges dotted with emerald lakes, deep forests broken by meandering rivers, and gentle hills interrupted by large, crystal-clear lakes. Located in the heart of Europe, Bavaria's long history can be traced in the architecture of its monuments, echoing the influence of other peoples, wars and glories. The Celts, Romans, French and Austrians have all had their turn at dominating this territory, which takes its name from the Baiuvarii, the Germanic tribe that first settled here. Every culture left its mark on the countryside, in the culture and in the cuisine of Bavaria, but throughout its long, intricate history, the events which probably most affected its modern-day appearance were two major conflicts: the Thirty Years' War and the Second World War. The bigotry and persecution practised by Catholics and Protestants during the Reformation finally erupted into one of the most devastating conflicts (both in terms of human life and artistic treasures) that Europe had ever known — the Thirty Years' War, which sucked France, Spain, Denmark and Sweden into its vortex of senseless violence.

8 top From the baroque gardens, the horseshoe-shaped staircase leads to the terrace where Linderhof Castle, Ludwig II's pleasant refuge in the valley of Graswang, stands.

8 bottom "Atlas upholding the world" dominates the tympanum of Linderhof's main facade. The Kingdom of Bavaria's coat of arms, upheld by two winged spirits, appears in the tympanum.

8-9 Ludwig II began construction of Neuschwanstein Castle in 1848 in one of the most beautiful areas of Bavarian Allgaü-Swabia, with the idea of creating the castle of the knights of the Holy Grail.

9 top In the park at Herrenchiemsee, fountains, geometrical hedges and statues depicting hunting scenes and mythological deities recreate the atmosphere of court gardens during the era of the Sun King.

10 top left Prunn Castle, with its incredible position, overlooks the tranquil Altmühl River.

10 centre left When new techniques of warfare made fortified defensive castles obsolete and the Renaissance breathed a new spirit of life throughout Europe, even the Bavarian nobles left their austere, uncomfortable fortresses

to build new palaces and residences with the luxuries of the new era. This photograph shows Nymphenburg Castle, the Wittelsbach family's summer residence.

10 bottom left The picture shows the Würzburg Residenz. With their love for architecture and the fine arts, the von Schönborn family of bishop princes

embellished innumerable cities of Bavaria, including Neuburg, Bamberg and Würzburg.

10 top right Located in a picturesque setting and surrounded by water, Mespelbrunn Castle is a perfect example of a fortified structure which over the centuries was transformed into an elegant residence.

After the war, it took Germany forty years to recover from the resulting social and economic collapse (almost a third of the population had been killed). The Wittelsbach family, however, whose name runs like a thread throughout the history of Bavaria, embarked on the great task of rebuilding their land.

As the result of the long war, trading and communication difficulties and an even longer period of recovery, the whole country thus made the transition from the Gothic period directly to the baroque, almost entirely skipping the Renaissance, which left only rare traces throughout most of Germany. In effect, the new style coming from Italy, so exuberant, rich and sensual, was the perfect antidote to sober Protestantism and all the ugliness of the preceding conflicts.

Newly regained economic well-being made it possible to invest in the best artists of the period, and cities, castles and churches were rebuilt and restored in the new style, adapted to local taste, thus creating the Bavarian baroque.

Unfortunately, in the heat of the moment almost everything that had survived the past catastrophes was made baroque, and even though many Romanesque and Gothic buildings have survived to the present, it is extremely rare to find interiors which were not modified in accordance with the taste of the times.

Unfortunately, World War II left an indelible scar, as Bavaria was one of the areas in Germany with the greatest wealth of artistic treasures. Yet it can still astound us with the uniqueness and variety of its natural beauties and historic monuments.

In this book we have chosen to show Bavaria through the history and images of its fortresses and castles, which function as both a point of departure and a point of arrival in the history of a particular area, town or city. World-renowned for the castles of Ludwig II, Bavaria truly is a land of castles.

There are hundreds of ruins, with fortresses, fortifications, and royal residences that emerge everywhere out of the idyllic countryside as witnesses to the long history of Bavaria, its desire for independence and freedom and its pride in and awareness of its accomplishments. It was difficult to select only a few of these castles, because they all have an individual charm and a unique architecture, interior or position that make them worthy of being added to the most representative groups. We thus decided to divide them into three chapters unrelated to itineraries (although the castles are described in geographical order from south to north), and connect them by historical and architectural groups instead.

The castles of Ludwig II have their own chapter, because they are really not part of the history and architecture of their period, but rather from some sort of dreamtime. The other two chapters are dedicated to fortified castles and residential castles.

10-11 No longer merely a fortress, but a true fortified citadel that for many centuries was an impregnable buttress guarding the borders of lower Bavaria, the fortress of Burghausen, over one kilometre long, is the longest fortified castle in Germany.

11 top The fortress of Nuremberg played an important role in the history of both Bavaria and Germany, and historically and architecturally is one of the most important fortresses in Europe.

Neuschwanstein Castle.

Fränk. Saale

Coburg

Weisser Main

Aschaffenburg

Main

Roter Main

Bayreuth

Mespelbrunn

Bamberg

Würzburg

Pottenstein

Aisch

Naab

Nuremberg

Ansbach

Altmühl

Regen

Riedenburg

Eichstätt

Prunn

Harburg

Danube

Danube

Isar

Augsburg

Landshut

Passau

Rott

Wertach

Amper

Lech

Isar

Scleissheim

Munich

Burghausen

Inn

Ammersee

Herrenchiemsee

Starnberger
See

Chiemsee

Kempten

Füssen   Hohenschwangau

Neuschwanstein

Linderhof

Herrenchiemsee Castle.

Schleissheim Castle.

Nymphenburg Castle.

Harburg Castle.

Prunn Castle.

14-15 A marble staircase in the fairy-tale castle of Neuschwanstein leads to the gilt apse of the Throne Room, which contains the painting Christ in His Glory and representations of six canonized kings and the Twelve Apostles.

16-17 Kaiserburg, one of the most beautiful and imposing fortresses in Germany, has undergone many changes over the centuries. Its massive Sinwell Tower can be seen for miles.

THE DREAM OF LUDWIG II, "THE FAIRY-TALE KING"

Some of the most sumptuous and well-known castles in the world are certainly those of that symbol of Bavaria, Ludwig II, whose ministers consistently attempted to block their construction. These amazingly eccentric works, which have no parallel in the architecture of their time, were a product of the imagination and dreams of a monarch who was affectionately known as "The Fairy-Tale King" by his subjects, but was considered the "Mad King" by his ministers. To understand his castles, one must look at the life of Ludwig II. He was very young when he inherited the heavy burden of a throne which had previously been occupied by two great political figures: his grandfather, Ludwig I, and his father, Maximilian II, who had succeeded in making Munich the European capital of art and culture. Born on August 25, 1845 in the royal palace of Nymphenburg in Munich, he passed a lonely adolescence in the manor of Hohenschwangau. His mother, queen Marie, notes in her diary that the child appreciated art, built churches and castles with his wooden blocks, liked to dress up and was very generous with his toys. This natural character and the type of education he received made him a dreamer. Fantastic images of the historical past, German sagas and a love of the exotic steadily distanced him from reality. As he grew up, he became enamoured of the figure of the Sun King and the splendours of Versailles. His father's ideal of a consti-

tutional monarchy was totally contrary to the vision of absolute power and the passion for the Bourbons that had rooted in him. Another passion that caused no end of problems with his ministers was his love for Richard Wagner's music, which at that time was considered a hodgepodge of deafening sounds, discordant and even dangerous. As soon as he came to the throne, Ludwig II began to search for his hero, who had gone into hiding to avoid debts and had left his works incomplete. Thanks to the king's support and enormous monetary contributions, Wagner was able to complete his works, and his music gained international recognition. The veneration and love that the young Wittelsbach felt for the *maestro* were boundless, but unlike his grandfather, who preferred the love of Lola Montez to his reign, Ludwig did not have the necessary strength of character to oppose the orders of his Cabinet, which, worried about the "unbalancing" effect of Wagner's music and personality on the king, banished the artist from the court. The bond of affection between the brilliant composer and the restless monarch is evidenced in the letters the two exchanged, which in their exuberance and passion are not only some of the most revealing documents of the era, but are also a portrait of two unique, creative personalities. The great disappointment that this forced separation caused, besides continued opposition to his rare political decisions, caused him to distance himself

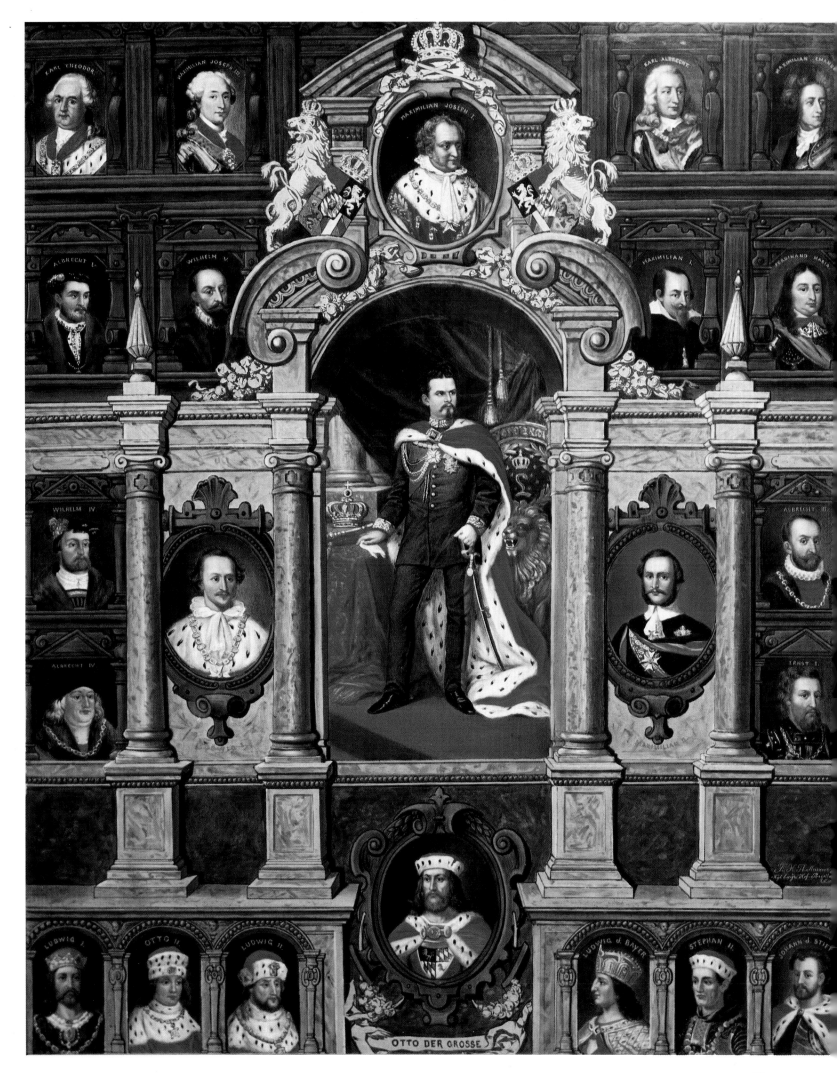

even farther from politics and to lose himself in his world of dreams. As he could not restore a reign of absolute power, he at least wanted to build a monument to himself. The resulting castles, which he himself designed and conceived, are the product of an unbridled imagination and a taste for the excessive and spectacular that only a king from times past could afford, combined with the period taste for mixing styles of past eras and the

increasingly frenzied. All this fed the imagination of the people, who loved his truly kingly excesses and adored him when, tall and handsome, he would come out of nowhere to share his lunch with a woodcutter, or knowledgeably discuss livestock with a shepherd. He was nevertheless quite shy and reserved and hated court occasions. He had very few friends, and the only woman in his life was his cousin Elizabeth, the empress of Austria, known as "Sisi". There was a deep platonic love between the two, who understood each other and shared confidences. Elizabeth was herself a strange character, and like the king was a great aesthete who was obsessed with her beauty. While Ludwig always carried his helmet under his arm so as not to crush his curls, the Austrian empress was obsessed with her weight and constantly engaged in physical activity and diets. Ludwig became engaged to Sisi's younger sister Sophie, perhaps to stop gossip about his relationship with Elizabeth, who was already the empress of Austria, or to put an end to more serious rumours about his homosexuality, but he broke off the engagement only 15 days before the wedding, when the sumptuous coach for the marriage had already been prepared. It is now on display at the Nymphenburg Museum, along with Ludwig's numerous other coaches. But it was neither scandals nor the king's eccentric behaviour that finally prompted his ministers to place the

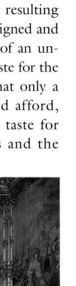

king's personal passion for German mythology and exotic settings. The king was not so much a madman as he was an eccentric dreamer, with the power, position and money to satisfy his whims and make his imaginary realm a reality. He loved to dress in the costumes of his legendary heroes, and would depart on nighttime runs on his gilded sleigh, accompanied by his faithful mounted escort. His bizarre behaviour accelerated along with his strange deeds, which became

20-21 Like a magician's spell, the white pinnacles of Neuschwanstein Castle rise out of the early morning mist.

21 top Linderhof Castle, with its pale colour and rounded facade, fountains and baroque garden covered with a blanket of snow, almost seems a natural part of the winter landscape.

22 and 23 Schachen Castle, built in the Alps near Garmisch-Partenkirchen, is actually a rustic mountain retreat which Ludwig II wanted for a hunting lodge. It nevertheless deserves to be called a castle because of its interior, which with the king's usual taste for opulence stands in sharp contrast to the simplicity of the exterior and is full of gilt and flourishing touches. Still, to maintain a little of the intimate and cozy atmosphere of a mountain refuge, the monarch furnished several rooms, such as the study (top right), the dining room (centre right) and the bedroom (bottom right) in a more simple and sober style.

king under judicial interdict, but rather his castles. In order to build and decorate them, Ludwig had gone into debt and had taken out loans of millions of marks from the Bank of Bavaria, and Linderhof and Herrenchiemsee had almost been repossessed by creditors. Yet it was impossible to dissuade the king from what he considered his mission. Citing the pretext that there was a strain of madness on his mother's side of the family (whose brother Otto was epileptic), the Cabinet had the king declared mentally infirm by a team of psychiatrists, whose judgement was then certified by an eminent luminary of the time who never examined the patient personally. Ludwig II was placed under house arrest at the castle of Berg on Starnberg Lake. On July 13, 1886, at the age of 40, overweight and suffering from the effects of tranquillizers and alcohol, he and his physician were found drowned on the banks of the lake that had been the scene of his few happy moments with his beloved cousin.

There are many theories on his death — some say it was a suicide (but why would his doctor have committed suicide too?), or that he tried to flee and was drowned (but he was an excellent swimmer), or that he was murdered because he had become too inconvenient. Whatever the explanation, his death was tragic and senseless. The empress Elizabeth, who was perhaps the only one who understood his soul, made this comment upon Ludwig's death: "The king was not mad; he was

only an eccentric who lived in a world of dreams. They should have treated him more gently..."; Paul Verlaine called him "the only true king of our century." The fruit of his romantic delirium, the castles of Neuschwanstein, Herrenchiemsee and Linderhof, spelled his disaster and his downfall but enriched the future of Bavaria with what are now the greatest tourist attractions not only in Bavaria, but in all of Germany.

NEUSCHWANSTEIN CASTLE

Neuschwanstein was the first of three castles begun in 1869, but was the last to be completed in 1886. Ludwig II did not enjoy it for long. In June of that same year he was deposed and left this castle for his last "escorted" trip to Berg, where he met his end.

This fairy-tale castle, which certainly inspired Walt Disney for his cartoons, was based on a childhood dream of the king that prompted him to create a utopian dwelling that would be both a medieval knights' castle and a temple to Wagner.

In his dream, the Swan Knight Lohengrin (in German *Schwan* means swan, which is why this creature recurs as a symbol and name) and the heroes of the Holy Grail spoke to him from the walls of Hohenschwangau Castle, while he eagerly gazed at the hill before it, hoping to capture the fleeting image of a true knight within the crumbling walls of the old medieval castle of Hinterschwangau. Wagner's music deeply touched Ludwig's mind and heart, but part of his attachment to the *maestro* was surely related to their mutual passion-obsession for German mythology. The period's romantic taste for restoring buildings in medieval style merged with his vision of the castle of the Swan Knight Lohengrin as he had seen him on the walls of his father's castle and heard him through the notes of Wagner's music. The astounding result of this dream was a castle so elaborate and perfect that it seems impossible to have been built by human beings using earthly materials, and more likely that divine hands placed it there overnight. Gleaming with a whiteness that stands out even from a distance, it seems to be resting on the treetops. Its five floors are interrupted by a myriad of towers, pinnacled turrets and columns that remind one of the sand castles children build by dribbling wet sand through their fingers. While the exterior is enchanting, the interior is hypnotic: silks, brocades,

24 top This photo shows a view from the west side of the castle, with its high octagonal tower and balcony inspired by that of Wartburg Castle.

24 bottom Neuschwanstein's brick entry is a contrast to the white winter world.

25 Neuschwanstein Castle emerges from the mists and clouds like a page in the legend of the Holy Grail.

26-27 Neuschwanstein Castle was never completed: the entire second floor, which is not open to the public, consists of empty rooms and bare brick walls.

lapis lazuli, gilt, bronze majolica, porcelains, marbles, and inlaid and engraved wood are used for all the architectural styles of the past — Gothic, Romanesque and Byzantine — but the sensation is never one of a hodgepodge, but rather the creation of yet another style, recognizable in all his Bavarian castles, which perhaps should be referred to as "Ludwigesque." Neuschwanstein Castle is perhaps the greatest example of 19th-century historicism, when Art Nouveau became the common thread joining the past eras that so greatly influenced the romantic spirit of the times.

What is more, all the king's projects made use of state-of-the-art techniques, with running water and complicated heating and special effects systems. Some stupendous examples include the grotto at Linderhof, the dinner table at Herrenchiemsee that can be raised and lowered through the floor to permit Ludwig to eat in solitude, and the kitchen at Neuschwanstein, ultramodern for its time. While Maximilian II and Ludwig I built primarily for the public, the castles of Ludwig II were for himself alone.

They were his very life, places where dream and reality merged and history came to life. As he wrote in a letter to Wagner, "in an ideal, monarchic and poetic solitude," he had tried to create an art in harmony with his personal ideal of the universe.

28 The white and blue colours of Bavaria stand out on one of the coats of arms that decorate the windows of the corridor.

28-29 Upon suggestion by Wagner, Ludwig II went to visit Wartburg Castle near Eisenach, the historical setting for the singing contest in Tannhäuser. *The king was so impressed by the castle that he wanted to recreate many of its moods in Neuschwanstein.*

29 top The most beautiful view of the fairy-tale castle is from the Maria Bridge. In the background is the village of Füssen.

*30 left This photo
shows the details of
one of the fanciful
painted friezes that
cover the walls of the
Singers' Room.*

*30-31 and 31 top
Two different angles
of the Singers' Room
show the beauty of the
caisson ceiling,
painted with*

*ornamental motifs
and the signs of the
zodiac, and the string
of brass candelabras
and candle holders
for over 600 candles.*

31 centre
The Singers' Room
ends with arcades
of marble columns
that frame
a representation
of the sorcerer
Klingsor's wood.
Above the arcades
are paintings of other
characters in the
Legend of Parsifal,
to whom the room
is dedicated.

31 bottom Paintings
which portray
moments in the life of
the young Parsifal
line the wall that
runs along the
corridor; this one
recounts the episode
in which the young
hero meets and kills
the Red Knight with
his boy's sword.

32 top The saga of Gudrun, Sigurd's widow, who would marry Attila and then assassinate him, is portrayed on the walls of the Waiting Room of the Singers' Room.

32 bottom
The central floor of the Throne Room is entirely in mosaic and includes ornamental forms and figures of plants and animals.

33 The two-level Throne Room is in the sumptuous style of a Byzantine church and is modelled after the All Saints' Church in Munich.

34 left top A painting depicting the meeting between Tannhäuser and Venus is shown on the walls of the King's Study.

34 bottom left The symbol of the castle, a white swan, stands on the delicate majolica stove. The word Schwan is in fact German for swan. The painting above depicts the arrival of Lohengrin.

34 top right A gilt bronze centrepiece depicting the battle between Siegfried and the Dragon stands on the richly inlaid table in the Dining Hall.

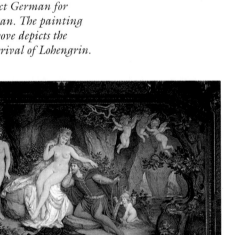

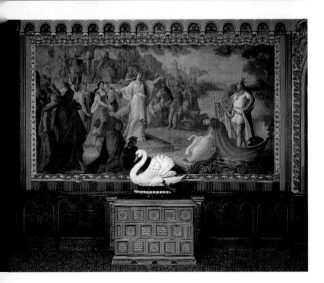

34 bottom right The Living Room is dedicated to the saga of Lohengrin, the Swan Knight, whose deeds charmed the young Ludwig and inspired the creation of the Neuschwanstein Castle. The mural above the sofa recounts the miracle of the Grail.

34-35 The Study is on the third floor, where the king's apartments are located; it is oak-panelled and filled with precious oak furniture. The ceiling is of inlaid wood and the saga of Tannhäuser is painted on the walls.

36 top These canvas paintings depict scenes described in the poetry of Walther van der Vogelweide and Hans Sachs.

36 centre As in all his other castles, Ludwig wanted his bed chamber to be especially sumptuous. In contrast with the other rooms in Romanesque style, this room is in late Gothic style.
The silver swan ewer over the wash basin is noteworthy.
The painting on the walls are dedicated to the poem of Tristan and Isolde.

36 bottom
The windows of the Royal Dressing Room look out over the upper courtyard.
The violet silk curtains are embroidered with peacocks, a beloved and recurring symbol in Ludwig II's castles.

37 The King's Oratorium is panelled in oak with neo-Gothic ornamentation.
The paintings on the walls, the windows and the central triptych represent Saint Louis, Ludwig II's patron saint.

38 top left Murals in the Waiting Room of the royal apartments on the third floor recount the legend of Sigurd, whose saga corresponds to the medieval saga of Siegfried; the version recounted in the Edda is the most ancient collection of Germanic legends in existence. This painting shows Regin as he forges the famous sword Gram for young Sigurd.

38 bottom left The old wise man Gripy foretells young Sigurd's destiny.

38 right Using a sword forged by the dwarf Regin, Sigurd kills Fafnir, who in the guise of a dragon guards the treasure taken from the Nibelungen.

39 This painting in the series painted by W. Hauschild in the Waiting Room of the Singers' Room, portrays King Attila courting Gudrun, Sigurd's widow.

LINDERHOF CASTLE

40 top left
The majolica vases
that adorn the
eastern flowerbeds
are of Nymphenburg
make, copied from
the originals from
Choisy-le-Roi.

40 bottom left
The photo shows one
of the two wrought
iron nymphs pouring
water into the little
fountain at the foot
of the first terrace on
the main parterre in
front of the palace.

The lovely Graswang Valley where Linderhof stands was a familiar place to the young Crown Prince. His father had already built a hunting lodge there, and when Ludwig II decided to build his Versailles, he originally planned it to be located near his castle at Linderhof. The original 1870 plan underwent many changes, and in the end Ludwig selected Lake Chiemsee for his Versailles project, building Herrenchiemsee Castle on an island in the lake. Linderhof, on the other hand, was designed to be a royal villa, while still keeping the look of Versailles. While it has been compared to the *Petit Trianon* and is decorated in eighteenth-century style, the castle's construction style is actually the only thing that resembles Versailles. It is the smallest of the three castles, with a more private, if not comfortable, touch. It is the only one of the three which the king saw to its conclusion in 1878, and where he lived most often and for the longest periods of time. The baroque and rococo interior is showy and ostentatious, full of gold and the brilliant blue which was the monarch's favourite colour. Swans and peacocks, Ludwig's two favourite animals, are one of its recurrent themes, as at his other castles, but only here does the royal coat of arms of Bavaria appear, both on the facade and in the interior. Despite its majesty and splendour, it was not intended as a state building, but rather as a retreat. While Herrenchiemsee was an ode to Louis XIV and

40 top right Karl von Effner, the director of the Royal Court Gardens, created the artistic design for the gardens in the north and south portions of Linderhof, following the models of the Italian Renaissance. Before the castle, the water from the fountain with its gilt zinc "Flora and Putti", spurts up to 30 metres high.

40 bottom right Right behind the palace, a little panoramic temple overlooks a flight of thirty marble steps. At its feet is the wrought iron fountain of Neptune and a large flowerbed in the form of a Bourbon lily.

41 Linderhof Castle is a small, splendid structure in rococo style that is one of Ludwig II's most elegant creations.

43 top Behind the fountain entitled "Cupid Shooting His Arrows", a leafy pavilion protects the stone bust of Louis XVI, to whom Ludwig felt bound by a certain kinship, as the king of France had baptized Ludwig I, Ludwig II's grandfather and godfather.

Neuschwanstein a celebration of Wagner and his muses, Linderhof was where the king most clearly expressed his desire to retreat into his fantasy world, where he alone could be the actor and the audience. On the rises of the valley, around the central portion of the royal villa, the king built small structures that became his microscopic fantasy world. The Moorish pavilion and the Moroccan house exude the exotic atmosphere of *The Thousand and One Nights*; in the hunting lodge he could stretch out on animal skins and drink mead to become one of the deities of the Nibelungen; and the Venus Grotto became his Blue Grotto, where he sailed on a gilded, shell-shaped boat. The gardens provide a natural link between the rococo castle and the rugged majesty of the Alpine landscape. Following the example of the Italian Renaissance, he took advantage of the natural features of the terrain to build terraces and waterfalls that allowed the flowerbeds and English gardens to blend into the natural mountain setting.

*42 top left
The eastern parterre includes four semirectangular flowerbeds that surround a quatrefoil pond. In the centre is a gilt group of statues entitled "Fame". At the back of the garden is the "Cupid with Dolphins", the central group of another small fountain. A terracotta bust of Louis XIV, whom Ludwig II considered an ideal absolute monarch, can be seen in the pavilion that closes off the garden.*

*42 bottom left
The photo shows one of the innumerable limestone statues that adorn the gardens.*

*42 top right
The golden statue entitled "Fame" rises above the four-leaf clover-shaped fountain in the western parterre.*

42-43 The gilt zinc cupid in the fountain in the eastern parterre seems to be shooting one of his arrows toward Linderhof's east facade.

44 top left
The Moorish pavilion
was built by the
Berlin architect Karl
von Diebitsch for the
international Paris
Exposition in 1867.
Ludwig II bought it
for Linderhof's park
and had it rebuilt
and refurnished,
making changes that
satisfied his taste for
opulence.

44 bottom left
As described for the
set in the first act
of The Valkyrie, *here*
is the Hunting Hut,
where the king could
sink into the
mythological world
of his heroes in
The Ring of the
Nibelungen.

44 right
The magically
illuminated area
of Venus' Grotto is
a reproduction of
the inside of
Hörselberg, the scene
of the first act of
Wagner's
Tannhäuser, but the
pool illuminated
from below draws its
inspiration from the
Blue Grotto at Capri.

45 The king of
Bavaria's passion
for the exotic was
completely gratified
in the "Thousand and
One Nights"
atmosphere of the
Peacock Room in the
Moorish pavilion. The
tails of the enamelled
wrought-iron peacocks
are studded with
hundreds of Bohemian
glass stones.

46-47 *A product of the cooperation between the architect Georg Dollmann and the set painter Joseph de la Paix, the model for the Room of Mirrors at Linderhof was the Mirror Room in the Rich Rooms of the Munich Residenz.*

47 top *The theme of the Music Room is "The Courtly Festivals," as shown in the large canvas paintings by H. von Pechmann, which depict pastoral and social scenes. The group of stucco putti above the doors are signed by Schmidt.*

47 bottom *Like Herrenchiemsee, Linderhof Castle is richly furnished. The passion for exquisitely made objects and furniture made Ludwig 11 a true patron of his time for artists and craftsmen from both Germany and abroad. The clock in the photo is Swiss, and the vases are of Meissen porcelain.*

48 Despite the intimate, cosy nature that Ludwig desired for Linderhof, he was unable to resist adding the central halls for court ceremonies, because he thought they were visual proof of an absolute monarchy. In the Audience Room there are in fact clear references to the kingdom of Bavaria in the stucco lunettes and above the throne's baldachin.

48-49 The painting on the left back wall of the Music Room is entitled "Pair of Shepherds at the Fountain", while that on the right is "Shepherd Girls with Bagpipe Player". The musical instrument is an aeolodion, a combination of a piano and a harmonium. In the centre is a life-size painted Sèvres porcelain peacock.

49 top The paintings in the East Tapestry Room, like those in the Music Room, were done on rough canvas to give a tapestry effect. The dark door frames are not ebony, but a special black marble from Belgium.

49 bottom A two-winged staircase, a smaller version of the Ambassadors' Stairway at Versailles, leads to the upper floor. In the centre is a Sèvres vase which the emperor Napoleon III is said to have given to Ludwig II.

50-51 The Bed Chamber in the Rich Rooms of the Munich Residenz was used as a direct model for the Bed Chamber at Linderhof, which is shown in the picture. Despite their similarities, in particular the bed alcove with its magnificent gold embroidery, there are significant differences, especially in the frescoed ceiling of Linderhof, which does not appear in Cuvilliés' original model.

52-53 A triumph of luxury, Herrenchiemsee Castle rises out of a dense wood on Herreninsel, the largest island on Lake Chiemsee.

52 top The facade of the castle that was inspired by Versailles can be seen among the sprays of water from the fountains. The castle is even more sumptuously furnished than its model in France.

HERRENCHIEMSEE CASTLE

_L_udwig's last great and most ambitious plan was to build a palace that was a replica of Versailles. His dream was to build the royal palace on the site of a modest hunting lodge built by his father near Linderhof, and over a period of five years the architect Georg Dollmann submitted thirteen designs for this "Meicost Ettal" (an anagram for "-L'état c'est moi," the motto of Louis XIV). In 1873, based on the last design, which exceeded the original Versailles in size, Ludwig decided to build the palace on the island of Herrenchiemsee on Lake Chiemsee, just a few kilometres north of Munich. He did not simply copy the French royal palace, but used it as a model for the most typical portions of the structure: the facade, the Ambassadors' Stairway and the king's state apartment. While Versailles is a conglomerate of structures from different periods, Herrenchiemsee was immediately conceived as a unitary system. Based on antique engravings, the Ambassadors' Stairway, which had been demolished in France in 1752, was reconstructed in Ludwig's palace and inserted symmetrically in its two wings.

The facade is larger than that of Versailles, and the Hall of Mirrors and rooms are also larger than the original. The sumptuous baroque bed chamber is different from the original, as is the so-called Small Apartment, a series of rooms not part of the original Versailles. These rooms were designed in Louis XV style, in

53 top The Fountain of Latona is a copy of the original at Versailles. The Statue of Latona overlooks the steps, where there are peasants transformed into frogs, with cast lead turtles and amphibians farther down.

53 bottom The great Fountain of Fame, a copy of a fountain in San Idelfonso in Spain, overlooks the north pond. There are

numerous mythological and allegorical figures in cast lead both on the rock and on the edge of the pond.

54 top The oval windows in the frieze area have given the second antechamber its name, the so-called Oeil de Boeuf Room, which is similar to that at Versailles. There is a small bronze statue of Louis XIV in the middle of the room. The paintings on the walls are also dedicated to the Sun King.

54 bottom The great hanging lamp with 108 candles, the centrepiece, the vases and the clocks of the Dining Hall are all in Meissen porcelain. As at Linderhof, due to the king's excessive sense of privacy, the table was lowered down through the floor and sent back up after it was set and prepared.

55 In the Vestibule, divided by columns and pillars, on an extraordinary floor of coloured marble, stands a monumental vase of Italian marble, with a pair of peacocks in bronze and translucent enamel. Along with the swan, the peacock was Ludwig II's emblem.

56-57 The Hall of Mirrors, based on a design by Georg Dollmann, is 98 metres long, even longer than the one at Versailles. Ludwig II tried to bring the Galerie des Glaçes back to its full splendour by reconstructing furnishings that had been lost for centuries.

an intentional contrast with the other rooms. The difference in style of the rooms is also due to the fact that the architect changed; Dollmann finished the state rooms and staircase in 1881, and in 1884 Julius Hofman took over to complete the king's rooms. Another significant difference is that at Versailles the rooms have no furniture, as it was destroyed and stolen during the revolution, while Herrenchiemsee is fully furnished.

As he had no models to imitate, all the furniture, porcelain, curtains, bronzes and clocks are original creations of the architects (whose designs the king himself often corrected and completed), who could indulge in their creative fancies through the

skilled artisans of Munich. Seven years of work were necessary on the parade chamber bed alone. Herrenchiemsee Castle should not be considered incomplete; even its original 1870 plan did not provide for any rooms within it other than those which are complete today. In order to celebrate his "absolute monarchy," all Ludwig needed or wanted were the rooms of Versailles. Herrenchiemsee is not a residence, but a monument, a stage for the works of a king who was born too late and could play his role only in fantasy, on an island that could be reached only by boat, far from the banalities of life.

58 centre left
A detail of the "Astronomy and History" panel shows a putto holding up a medallion with a portrait of Ludwig II. This is the only such panel in the whole castle, because the doors were not completed until after the king's death.

58 top and 58-59
The fireplace in the Porcelain Room is of Tunisian marble. The mirror, the hanging lamp, the candelabras, the vases, the clocks and the splendid console tables with delicately painted putti are all in precious Meissen porcelain.

58 bottom
This panoramic photo shows the Porcelain Room in all its elegance and richness. The ceiling is stuccoed, with a fresco representing the Spirit of Art. The precious desk is made of rosewood, with painted Meissen porcelain surfaces.

58 centre right
This is another detail of the room, showing one of the paintings with a mythological theme that duplicate the originals hanging in a room at Fontainebleau Palace.

60 centre left
In this painting by Ludwig Behringer (1864), the king is shown on horseback surrounded by his officials.

60 bottom
The halberds of the king's bodyguard are displayed amid the marble busts of the Sun King's marshals.
The Bodyguard Room is modelled after the Salle des Gardes, *and along with two other antechambers, the Bed Chamber, the Council Room and the Hall of Mirrors, it is one of the state rooms which were not part of the king's residence.*

60 top The walls in the Hall of Peace are of marbleized coloured stucco. A portrait of Louis XIV can be seen above the green Spanish marble fireplace. One of Herrenchiemsee's peculiarities is the oak floors with ornamental rosewood marquetry.

60 centre right
The monumental staircase is modelled after the Ambassadors' Stairway at Versailles, which was demolished in 1752. The coloured marble and marbleized stucco walls are a faithful duplication of the original, while the stairway at Versailles did not have the glass ceiling. The stucco figures in the niches were to have been of Vipiteno marble. Every time Ludwig came to the castle, the stairway was transformed into a carpet of flowers.

61 The Small Gallery ends the series of rooms that make up the royal apartments. The Rooms are based on the Small Gallery at Versailles, which no longer exists. There are allegorical stucco figures in the niches and above the main cornice.

62 centre Louis XIV was known for using his bed chamber for the first and last audiences of the day. The sumptuous State Room, which Ludwig II never used, is Herrenchiemsee at its most opulent. The Jörres and Bornhause workshops in Munich worked for seven years on the parade chamber bed alone.

62 bottom
The overflowing Blue Room is totally covered with relief decorations of gilt birds in iridescent colours. Mirrors are inserted into the panels so that the room seems to repeat itself endlessly.

62-63 Ludwig II's favourite colour, blue, is used for the baldachin, the curtains and the silk and velvet coverings inlaid with gold in the king's Bed Chamber. The headboard of the sumptuous inlaid wood bed depicts the sun that symbolized Louis XIV. A blue ball used to illuminate the room at night stands on a gilt stand with beautiful inlay work.

62 top Luxury abounds in the King's Study as well, which is furnished with rare and priceless objects which are masterpieces of artistic craftsmanship. The great roll-top desk is a copy of the famous Bureau du Roi on display at the Louvre. The spectacular silver and gilt bronze Elephant Clock stands on one console table along with two other elaborate astronomical clocks.

64 top The photo shows the Orangerie of the Kempten Residenz in this capital of the Bavarian Allgaü. The Residenz complex is one of the earliest examples of baroque architecture. The old residence of the abbot princes was designed by Beer in 1651 and was built over a number of years. Its interior clearly shows the transition from baroque decoration to rococo style.

64 bottom The Cathedral and the church tower of St. Lorenz, the largest baroque church in Germany, overlook the artistic gardens in the complex of ecclesiastical buildings that includes the Kempten Residenz. The church was built between 1652 and 1666 by M. Beer and J. Serro.

64-65 Neuburg Castle is a Renaissance work which overlooks this city on the Danube. During the 16th century, the Palatine Count Ottheinrich ordered the building of a three-winged structure in decorative Renaissance style on the site of a residential dwelling of the previous century.

A s the dark years of the Middle Ages drew to a close, albeit much more slowly than in southern Europe, the scent of the Renaissance managed to permeate even Germany. Bavaria, with a spirit more akin to southern Europe than to the rest of the country, absorbed it quickly. Its cramped fortresses made it impossible to live comfortably, and the need for comfortable quarters suitable for entertaining had grown so rapidly that princes and nobles found it impossible to live in those damp old fortifications, which by now had become useless as a means of defence against more modern techniques of war. The Thirty Years' War interrupted the construction of residences more in line with aristocratic needs, but the 17th century marked the advent of residential castles and dwellings. The rivalry among the various nobles families, among the families of bishop princes, and between bishops and the nobility exploded in a race to see who could build the most sumptuous, ostentatious dwelling. The architectural style in fashion in Italy — opulent, theatrical and fanciful — was the perfect response to the ferment that was enlivening the souls of Bavarian nobles. Counts, dukes and bishop princes began to build airy palaces (in total contrast to the dark, cramped rooms of defensive fortresses) in or near the cities, with entire suites of rooms and richly furnished salons surrounded by fairy-tale parks with enchanting additional structures, such as orangeries, pavilions and little temples. Baroque taste spread in all new buildings (and in most of the old ones too), followed by a lighter, more airy and even more whimsical rococo. Thus, residential castles appeared at the dawn of the modern era, united by their style of magnificent showiness, but each with the personal imprint of those who wanted to leave a permanent mark of their power and fame.

65 top Located among the forests and vineyards of Steigerwald, the splendid baroque palace of Pommersfelden is entirely decorated with elaborate frescoes. Its elegant architecture is still almost completely intact. The palace was built around the same time as the Würzburg Residenz and the New Residence of Bamberg.

THE MUNICH RESIDENZ

The superb Residenz stands on the central Max Josef Platz, where it was built on order of Maximilian I and his son Ludwig I. Once the family home of the Wittelsbach family, it is now one of the most splendid museums of the world. When the Swedes conquered Munich during the Thirty Years' War, King Gustav Adolf, admiring the Residenz, is said to have murmured, "If only it had wheels!" The Swedes not only did not carry it off, but their king's admiration for the splendid royal palace saved it from serious damage. Today, the Residenz is considered one of the most beautiful Renaissance palaces in Europe, although the buildings that crowd around the seven inner courtyards date from the 16th to 19th centuries and are a mixture of all the different styles that alternated during those centuries: Renaissance, baroque, rococo and neoclassical. After the bombardments of the Second World War, the complex had to be almost entirely rebuilt, but most of its sumptuous furnishings were saved and have now been returned to their original positions in the rooms. The sections open to the public constitute the *Residenzmuseum*. The *Alte Residenz*, with its entrance on Residenzstrasse, contains the main court sectors, including the splendid *Altes Residenztheater*, the rococo jewel of architect François de Cuvilliés. The *Königsbau*, with its Renaissance facade built in imitation of the Palazzo Pitti, was commissioned by Ludwig I and now serves as the entry to the Residenzmuseum. The more re-

66 top The Residenz, the Wittelsbach family's residential palace, is considered one of the most beautiful Renaissance palaces in Europe, even though the buildings that stand around seven inner courtyards are a combination of Renaissance, rococo and neoclassical styles. The facade on Max Josepf Platz was built between 1826 and 1833 by Leo von Kleuze, using the Palazzo Pitti and the Palazzo Rucellai as models.

66 centre Between 1581 and 1586, Duke Wilhelm V ordered the building of the Grottenhof, a structure with four wings and a richly decorated inner garden. Despite changes made, this "garden of secret delights" still exudes the joyous spirit of the Renaissance gardens of southern Europe.

66 bottom The Cave Room, covered in volcanic lava studded with shells, crystals and coloured rocks, opens onto the Grottenhof.

66-67 The Brunnenhof, or Court of Fountains, is a long octagon which was created between 1612 and 1616 by joining new buildings to already existing sections. The Wittelsbach Fountain, which stands in the centre, honours the first duke of the dynasty, Count Otto von Wittelsbach, whose bronze statue is upheld by the four elements and the four river deities.

67 top This photo shows the south façade of the Residenz, with the statue of Max Joseph Denkmal in the foreground. Unfortunately, what we see of the Residenz today is mostly a faithful reconstruction: the bombardments of 1945 destroyed this masterpiece of five centuries of Bavarian history in just a few hours.

68 top In 1726, under the supervision of Joseph Effner, the Great Garden Room was remodelled as the Ancestors' Gallery. The 121 portraits immortalize the rulers of Bavaria, primarily the Wittelsbachs and their relatives up to 1913. The gilt stucco work on the ceiling is by Johann Baptist Zimmermann.

cent north wing — built between 1837 and 1842 and known as the *Festsaalbau* — contains the *Herculessaal*, now a concert hall. The *Hofgarten*, a magnificent courtyard garden, was embellished during the reign of Maximilian I with porticoes and a little round temple with an interesting frescoed cupola.

The oldest portions of the palace are the *Grottenhof*, built under William V in 1585 as a "garden of secret pleasures," and the *Antiquarium* (ordered by Albrecht V in 1568 to hold the Wittelsbach collection of antiquities), the work of Jacopo Strada and the most important Renaissance period secular construction north of the Alps. The most spectacular and extravagant rooms of the royal palace are on the upper floor. The *Reiches Zimmer* represent another splendid piece of German rococo by François de Cuvilliés, decorated with stucco work by Johann Baptist Zimmermann. They lead to the Secret Chapel, a niche gleaming with gilt and lapis lazuli decorations, with floors and walls covered with mosaics of marble and coloured stone.

68 centre The wall decorations in the Throne Room are astonishing and unique: the walls below the marbleized stucco panels are totally gilt with a network of palm-shaped decorations.

68 bottom The Imperial Room measures 34 metres by 15 and is 10 metres high. The central paintings on the ceiling, which burned in 1944, have been replaced by scale model photographic reproductions. The paintings above the windows were done in Venice by Andrea Vicentino. Fifteen wool tapestries depict heroes of the Old Testament.

68-69 The Reiche Kapelle *concludes the sequence of Rich Rooms in the Residenz. The ceiling is decorated in gilt stucco work on an azurite background. Many scagliola decorations, the altar, the eight windows, and numerous reliquaries and statuettes were saved from the bombardments.*

69 top The Altes Residenztheater, or Cuvilliés Theatre, is the rococo triumph of the great Belgian architect and former court jester François de Cuvilliés. The Elector Max Emanuel discovered the dwarf's talent for design as soon as he arrived at court, and sent him to Paris to study.

70-71 The most important and, at 66 metres long, the largest secular Renaissance room north of the Alps, the Antiquarium *was created by Jacopo Strada and Simon Zwitzel under Duke Albrecht V between 1568 and 1571 for the dukes' collection of antiquities.*

SCHLEISSHEIM CASTLE

Schleissheim Castle is located in Oberschleissheim, about 20 kilometres from central Munich. This splendid baroque complex consists of two palaces built one in front of the other. The first, known as the Old Castle, was begun in 1597 as a modest residence for Duke Wilhelm V, based on a design by Heinrich Schön. In 1616 his son, Duke Maximilian I, took it over, and the "refuge" grew into an Italian Renaissance-style palace. Unfortunately, today's structure is only a pale shadow of what it was before the bombardments of World War II destroyed it. Only the outside has been reconstructed, but inside you can still admire an interesting exhibit of "domestic" religious objects like Nativity cradles, representations of the Passion and Easter eggs from eastern Europe.

The Old Castle is obscured by the grandiose New Castle. As early as 1693, the Elector Maximilian II Emanuel decided to expand the existing residence. The work was first directed by Enrico Zuccalli. The War of Spanish Succession put a stop to work until 1719, and Joseph Effner (a Bavarian architect who had studied in France) was commissioned to continue with the project following new plans. Effner hired great names in the architecture of the time, including François de Cuvillés, Johann Baptist Zimmermann and Cosmas Damian Asam, who became involved in a frenetic whirl of creativity. The New Castle was completed between 1847 and 1848, but the connection to the Old Castle which was to have completed the whole structure was never finished. Without counting the galleries and side pavilions, the main building's facade alone measures fully 330 metres in length and is covered with precious late baroque ornamentation.

From the opulent ground floor, completely decorated in stucco work and frescoes and dotted with red marble columns, a magnificent staircase leads to the first floor where the *Barockgalerie* contains the most important collection of baroque paintings in Germany.

Even surrounded by all this magnificent baroque art, the *Grosser Saal* still takes the breath away, with a dazzling splendour only slightly dimmed by the superb paintings of Jacopo Amigoni that cover the ceiling with scenes from the history of the Wittelsbach family. The wonderful summer concerts of Schleissheim take place in this hall.

The elegant, French-style gardens, which are absolutely idyllic and a perfect setting for the buildings, are adorned by arabesques of a variety of flowers and coloured rocks, geometrical hedges and canals with waterfalls. They were embellished by Joseph Effner and Dominique Girard in 1715. Within them rises *Gartenschloss* Lustheim (the Garden Palace), a lovely little castle built as a wedding gift for Maria Antonia, the wife of the prince. It was designed by Zuccalli as well. Its light, delicately decorated rooms contain one of the most beautiful collections of porcelain in Europe, the *Meissner-Porzellansammlung*, which blends in superbly with the baroque interior.

73 The scagliola decorations and marbleized stucco work give the New Castle's chapel an embroidered effect. The gilt stucco work on the ceiling frames the opening to an upper level.

74 The large
Tapestry Room is
covered with precious
silk tapestries
depicting battle
scenes. The wooden
furniture is carved
and gilt, and the
porcelain objects
are of Nymphenburg
make.

75-78 The elegant
profile of the New
Castle stands out
against the clear
sky of Bavaria. Rich
furnishings and the
art gallery, with
works from the 16th
to 18th centuries,
give an idea of 18th-
century court life.

79 Following the Sun King's custom of holding his first and last audiences of the day in the bed chamber, a State Bed Chamber was also prepared at Schleissheim, with an alcove covered in purple silk and velvet interwoven with gold thread.

NYMPHENBURG CASTLE

Magnificent Nymphenburg Castle at the gates of Munich was the summer residence of Bavarian royalty until 1918. The spacious complex, whose most noteworthy feature is the large group of separate buildings connected by an absolute symmetry of line, is the result of various phases of work. Its development over the centuries is the result of the creativity of four generations of Wittelsbachs. The oldest part of the palace, the five-storey central pavilion, was built in 1662 by prince Ferdinand Maria, when his wife, Adelaide of Savoy, gave birth to his heir after 10 years of waiting. The sumptuous edifice was designed by the Italian architect Agostino Barelli. Subsequently, the central portion of the palace and the magnificent double stairway at the entrance were designed by Enrico Zuccalli. Adelaide's son Max Emanuel inherited the castle, and in 1704, with the aid of Joseph Effner, he added the final touches that give the palace its present-day appearance: two Italian-style side villas, joined to the two wings of the main building, the court stables, the waterfall in the park, and the *Badenburg*, *Pagodenburg* and *Magdalenenklause* pavilions. During the reign of Karl Albrecht VII, the little villas for court nobles were built around the artificial lake in the courtyard facing the palace; since 1747 they have housed the famous Nymphenburg Porcelain Factory. In the park is the stupendous *Amalienburg*, a hunting lodge the Emperor ordered in honour of his wife Amalia.

80 top This photo shows a detail of the facade of the central pavilion at Nymphenburg, remodelled by the Elector Max Emanuel using late French baroque ornamental motifs.

80 bottom The photo is a view of the Rondell Bauten. Effner's design enlarged the palace by adding a vast semicircular cour d'honneur *in front of the main building. It was designed to include the Elector's stables and apartments for officials. Cuvilliés was responsible for executing the design, working under Karl Albrecht.*

80-81 The oldest part of Nymphenburg Castle is the central pavilion with its five floors. The old summer home had been built in 1664 by Adelaide of Savoy, the wife of the Elector Ferdinand Maria. The romantic princess dedicated the palace to the goddess Flora as "a place for recreation and pastoral pleasures."

81 top The Magdalenenklause *pavilion consists of false ruins with feigned poverty meant to imitate the cells of hermits. Built in the middle of the park, it represents a desire to take refuge in solitude and escape formal court life.*

*82 and 82-83
Classical art and
feminine beauty were
the two great passions
of Ludwig I, Ludwig
II's grandfather.
To pay homage
to the women
in his life, the king
commissioned Joseph
Stieler to paint them
in 36 marvellous
portraits displayed
in the Gallery
of Beauties.
The portraits show*

*the following women
in all their splendour:
Lady Theresa Spencer
(top left), Caroline
von Holnstein (bottom
left), Marie of Prussia,
mother of Ludwig II
(top right), Helena
Sedelmayer, daughter
of a shoemaker
(centre right), the
famous adventuress
Lola Montez (bottom
right) and Sophie von
Österreich, Ludwig I's
half-sister.*

François de Cuvilliés, with the help of stucco work by Johann Baptist Zimmermann and wood decorations by Joachim Dietrich, ensured that even the splendour of the castle's Hall of Mirrors would pale in comparison with the interior of *Amalienburg*.

Maximilian Joseph III further embellished the palace, changing and redecorating many rooms. He also made use of the genius of Zimmermann and the elderly Cuvilliés, and gave the *Steinerner Saal* (Marble Hall) that sumptuous atmosphere that still enchants the spectators who come to summer concerts at Nymphenburg.

Another fascinating room is the extraordinary Gallery of Beauties, a collection of thirty-six portraits of the most beau-

tiful women of the period, painted by Joseph Stieler on commission by Ludwig I. Like his son and grandson, Ludwig I had great aesthetic taste, and like his grandson, his love of beauty caused him to lose his reign.

While Ludwig II's battles with his Cabinet were due to his castles, Ludwig I's problems in governing were due to the beauties of his gallery. Lola Montez, an adventuress of common origins, may not have been the most beautiful of the women in the portraits, but she was certainly the most intelligent. She had great political and personal influence over the king, whose government forced him to exile her. Thereafter, Ludwig I fell into a deep depression and abdicated in 1848.

*83 top left
The splendid effect
of this party room,
the Steinerner Saal,
is the result of Effner's
skilled use of space,
with walls broken
by pillars that support
the almost square
vault. During the
reign of Maximilian
Joseph III, Cuvilliés
divided the part
overlooking the
garden into two floors.
The frescoes were done
by the 76 year-old
Johann Baptist
Zimmermann.*

*83 top right
The Gallery of
Beauties is in the
former Small Dining
Room in the
apartments of Queen
Caroline, the wife
of Max Joseph I.
The gallery contains
portraits of not only
noblewomen, but
women of every social
level, bound only by
their special allure.*

84 top During his renovation work on the park near Badenburg in 1769, the landscape architect Friedrich Ludwig von Sckell created the Badenburgsee, a little lake with a small Greek-style temple.

84 centre Badenburg, unique among its kind, was built by Effner as a small bathing pavilion for Max Emanuel. The photo shows the Banquet Room, with decorations inspired mostly by agriculture and water. The frescoes are by Jacopo Amigoni, the only ones in Nymphenburg by this Italian artist, who was employed primarily for the frescoes on the ceiling of Schleissheim Castle.

84 bottom Badenburg consists of three large rooms (besides the small baths and the kitchen in the basement): the Banquet Room, the Bed Chamber and the Bathing Room, which is actually a small but sumptuous swimming pool on two levels of the structure.

84-85 Created as a little hunting lodge for the Elector Amalia between 1734 and 1739, elegant Amalienburg is another splendid project by Cuvilliés. Built in the landscaped garden like the other pavilions, its interior decoration is important due to the artistic effect created by the suite of rooms and the profuse ornamentation.

85 top left The Mirror Room at Amalienburg is the culmination of the interior decoration within Nymphenburg. Zimmermann did the stucco work, which has a silvery hue that gives a rare lightness to such elaborate and dense ornamentation. The exquisite scheme of silver and blue repeats itself endlessly in the refined play of mirrors.

85 top right The kitchen at Amalienburg, is artistically decorated as well: the walls are all entirely covered with white and blue or brightly coloured Dutch tiles which form magnificent vases of flowers or depict scenes of daily life in China.

86 and 87 top left The Marstallmuseum building, where a superb collection of gala coaches from the Wittelsbach family is housed, is located south of the Nymphenburg complex. Some of its most precious pieces include the coaches and sleighs of Ludwig II, with the spectacular coach the king had built for his marriage to Sophie, Sisi's sister; the marriage was called off and the coach was never used.

87 top right In the restful atmosphere of the Pagodenburg *Living Room, the white and blue colour scheme of the Dutch tiles that cover the walls is repeated on the floor, in the paintings on the ceiling and in the furniture.*

87 centre right The pavilions of the princely summer residence were intended to provide a place of seclusion from incessant court activities, as well as exotic atmospheres that would give the impression of being in distant lands. On the outside, the Pagodenburg *is simple, almost austere, but its interior is richly furnished for exclusive parties and exudes an atmosphere of the far-off Orient.*

87 bottom right The three rooms on the upper floor of the Pagodenburg *are decorated with Oriental motifs. This is one of the Chinese Rooms, with black lacquered panels and painted silk and rice paper.*

ANSBACH CASTLE

Ansbach, a pearl of baroque and rococo style, is the capital of Rangau, the central region of Franconia, on the border of the Land of Baden-Württemberg. The city grew up within the Benedictine monastery founded by St. Gumbert in 748. In 1381, the city was taken over by the Burgraves of Nuremberg, the Hohenzollern family, who used it to extend the dominion of Ansbach-Bayreuth. A little later, it was chosen as the residence of one of the dynastic branches, and a splendid fortress on

water was built there as the residence of the Von Brandeburg-Ansbach Margraves. The palace then underwent many renovations, until it was decided to build an entirely new residence.

In 1705 the architect Gabriel de Gabrieli (a native of Rovereto, Italy) was hired, but ten years later he left the job, which was continued by Leopoldo Retti of Como. The Margrave died, and the task of completing the ambitious work passed on to his widow. She expanded the original plan and created the park, the *Hofgarten* (Court Garden), where in memory of her husband she planted two rows of linden trees in the form of a cross. The magnificent Orangerie is located at the entrance to the gardens; today it is used as a concert hall. It was built in 1726 based on the model of two French architectural masterpieces: the side facing the gardens was inspired by the *Grand Trianon* of Versailles, while the other side was based on the Louvre. The gardens were also the scene of a dark and strange story, with a small stone marker showing the spot where, in 1883, Kaspar Hauser, a mysterious foundling inexplicably adopted by a rich English lord, was beaten to death for no apparent reason. The interior is in early rococo style, with delicate forms and colours. The *Festsaal* is extremely beautiful, embellished with stucco work and frescoes by Diego and Carlo Carlone, as are the brilliant *Spiegelkabinett* (Hall of Mirrors) and the priceless *Gekachelter Saal*, covered with 2800 ceramic tiles from Ansbach.

88 top The elegant facade of the Ansbach Residenz, crowned by a balustrade with statues and gracefully dotted with pillars, is the work of Gabriel de Gabrieli and Leopoldo Retti.

88 bottom Every important noble residence of the period had to have an opulent Hall of Mirrors. The Spiegelkabinett of the Ansbach Residenz was designed by J.C. Wezler in 1739, and in accordance with the baroque taste of the time is full of gilt and porcelain.

88-89 The Court Gardens lie to the southwest of the Residenz. At the entrance is the great Orangerie, based on the Grand Trianon of Versailles. The building, more than 100 metres long, is now used as a concert hall.

89 top One of the most noteworthy rooms in the Residenz is the Party Room, designed in 1737 by Leopold Retti. Its refined stucco work was done by one of the most important stucco artists of the time, Diego Carlone. The 250 metre ceiling of the two story room features an allegorical fresco by Carlo Carlone adulating the Margrave Carl Wilhelm Friederich, in the "good government" style thematized throughout art history.

90 top In the centre
of the large square,
dominating the main
entrance to the
Residenz, is the
Franconia Fountain,
with statues of great
men of the region,
including the sculptor
Tillman
Riemenschneider
(right) and Matthias
Grünewald,
a painter, architect
and hydraulic
engineer (left).

THE WÜRZBURG RESIDENZ

90-91
The magnificent
Residenz complex
consists of a central
structure and two
side wings. A
masterpiece
of German baroque,
the lordly residence
was built between
1719 and 1744 based
on a design by
Balthasar Neumann,
with the assistance of
Lukas von
Hildebrandt from
Vienna and M. V.
Welsch from Mainz.

W ürzburg is a lovely city located in a splendid position on the Main River, surrounded by hills covered with vineyards that reach the city centre. Its elegant eighteenth-century appearance survived the destruction of the Second World War, and its pearl is the Residenz, the most beautiful baroque castle in all of Germany, located in the eastern portion of the city. In 1720 the new bishop prince, Johann Philipp von Schönborn, decided that it was time to build a palace which was larger and more modern than the massive fortress of Marienberg, perched on the hill. By this time, it was no longer necessary to live in a fortified castle, and after the Thirty Years' War the city was experiencing a period of economic growth and had a great desire to rebuild and renovate. The Schönborns were a rich and influential family which had produced at least twelve bishops, all with a passion for building and the gift of good taste. Johann Philipp demonstrated incredible far-sightedness in selecting Balthasar Neumann as his chief architect. This young man who built cannon and bells and until then had designed only his own home, became one of the greatest German architects of his time, and thanks to his genius, the bishop prince realized his dream of building a "castle to excel all other castles," a grandiose sandstone building soaring up splendidly from its own square. A half a century later, Napoleon called it the most beautiful residence in Europe.

91 top This portrait
of Balthasar
Neumann hangs
in the Main and
Franconia Museum
in the Marienberg
fortress. In the
background one can
see his masterpiece,
the Residenz. The
Bohemian architect
is shown in armour,
resting on a cannon,
as he was a gunner
in the Episcopal
artillery: architecture
was only a hobby.

91 bottom
The insignia
of the bishop prince,
surrounded by
allegorical sandstone
statues, can be seen
above the main
entrance.

92 top June concerts have been held in the palace and park behind it since 1922 as part of the annual Festival dedicated to Mozart.

92-93 The garden side of one of the wings of the Residenz is shown here. As Johann Philipp von Schönborn wanted to move from the uncomfortable, cold Marienberg as soon as possible, work on the new castle proceeded with all due haste: more than 100 workers laboured continuously in the main building yards.

Two of Neumann's creations are visible as you enter the vestibule: the staircase and the ceiling, true miracles of static engineering. The ceiling (18 by 32 metres in size) covers the entire area of the grand staircase without the support of a single pillar. Everyone was sure it would collapse before completion, and one of Neumann's rival architects declared that he would hang himself from the ceiling if it held up. Irritated, Neumann asked the bishop prince to test the structure by firing cannon salvoes under it. No test was ever performed, but during the bombardment of 1945, when most of the Residenz was destroyed, the staircase and the ceiling survived. The ceiling is also famous for being the largest existing fresco in the world. It is the work of a genius of Italian painting, Gian Battista Tiepolo, who like many other Italian artists of the period was paid handsomely to bring the fashionable style of Italy to Germany. The artist, assisted by his two sons, took three years to complete the ceiling and the other frescoes in the Residenz.

Another Italian artist, Antonio Bossi, is responsible for the incredible stucco work in the *Weisser Hall* (the White Hall). Already at the edge of madness, Bossi unleashed his imagination in original, unique forms before succumbing permanently to his psychosis. The whiteness of this hall provides a rest for the eyes before entering the explosion of colours and gilt in the Imperial Hall. Here Bossi's stucco details provide a framework for the strange optical effects that Tiepolo created in his frescoes. Neumann's triumphs continue in the Court Chapel as well, a burst of spiral-shaped columns, curving balconies and intersecting arches, also embellished by Tiepolo's paintings. The Residenz's treasures do not lie only in its halls, but in its immense cellars as well, where some of the finest wines of Franconia are produced and aged.

The splendid Baroque Gardens, with the Residenz providing the background, are a yearly summer setting for a series of concerts dedicated to Mozart, as well as a lively Wine Festival featuring wine produced in its cellars.

96 left The photo shows the Audience Room with its great tapestries. An extremely elegant majolica stove can be seen in the corner.

96 top right The Hall of Mirrors was totally destroyed during the Second World War, but thanks to the painstaking work of highly specialized artists, it was totally restored.

96 bottom right The Green Room is entirely covered in exquisite lacquered rococo panels.

97 Antonio Bossi did the stucco work for the Residenz Chapel, a burst of columns, arches and gilt. The paintings on the altar of this small, opulent baroque church are by Tiepolo.

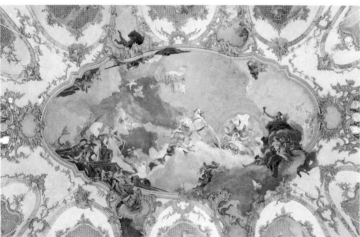

98 and 98-99
The artistic
partnership between
Bossi and Tiepolo
created an unusual
freedom of expression
in the Emperor's
Room. The stucco
artist has allowed
frescoes to appear
from behind the folds
of a curtain, as if on
a stage. On the edges,
a leg, a head, or a
cloud peeps out from
the frame, blurring
the distinction
between two- and
three-dimensionality.
The frescoes on
the sides of the walls
and on the ceiling
show various scenes,
including (bottom
left) the marriage
of Frederick
Barbarossa to
Beatrice of Burgundy,
and (in the picture
at right) the bishop
of Würzburg and
the duke of Franconia
discussing "good
government".

GIO. BTTA. TIEPO

*99 top
The Antechamber
of the Emperor's
Room, decorated
with bizarre
ornamentation and
sinuous rococo motifs
in white stucco, was*

*Antonio Bossi's last
work before he totally
succumbed to madness.
The room was
prepared just
in time for a visit
by the empress Maria
Teresa in 1745.*

100-101 The Garden Room, which opens out on ground level, was a "buffer zone" used for serving refreshments or as a place for musicians. Bossi hid mirrors within his stucco work that shine with a magical, mysterious light in the glow of the candles. The frescoes by Johann Zick show the contrast between rigid court formality and utopian rustic abandon. The main painting (bottom left) shows the "Banquet of the Gods".

THE NEUE RESIDENZ OF BAMBERG

L ike Rome, Bamberg bears the architectural mark of the secular power of the Church. On the hill that dominates the city centre, the same square holds two opposing examples of religious power: the cathedral, the house of God, with its solid and austere Gothic appearance and its four spires that seem to pierce the sky, represents the Church's power of guidance and salvation, while on the opposite side of the square, between the cathedral and the city, stands the sumptuous Residenz, the home of the bishop, symbol of the vanity and temporal power of the clergy. The Renaissance-style west wing was completed between 1605 and 1611 by the city of Nuremberg's architect, Jakob Wolff the Elder, by order of the bishop prince Johann Philipp von Gebsattel. The two baroque wings facing the cathedral were commissioned by the man described as "one of the most gifted and impulsive princes who ever

occupied the episcopal seat of Bamberg," the elector of Mainz, Lothar Franz von Schönborn (1693-1729). During the early years of his election, he had to restrain his mania for expanding and enriching his residence to meet the fashion of the time, because the cathedral Chapter had imposed a condition that formally forbade him from squandering finances in opulent buildings or improvements on already existing residences. When his insistent pressure finally resulted in a pontifical decree freeing him from this constraint, he immediately commissioned his architect, Leonhard Dientzenhofer, to design a new Residenz, which in six years became the building we can admire today. Inside the Neue Residenz is the State Library, with an exceptional collection of 4,500 manuscripts dating as far back as the 5th century, 3,400 incunabula and 70,000 drawings. The guided visit leads through the Grand Halls, full of magnificent furniture, porcelains and carpets, and the Imperial Hall, a large room which in reality has a rather low ceiling, but which uses perspective frescoes with optical illusions — by the court painter Melchior Steidl — to give an impression of openness and space. Enclosed within the wings of the Residenz is the *Rosegarten* (the Rose Garden), graced by the fragrance of a thousand varieties of roses, with bold statues by Ferdinand Tietz eternally overlooking the old roofs of the city below.

THE BAYREUTH HERMITAGE

104 left One of the great attractions of the Hermitage is the garden, considered one of the most beautiful English gardens in Germany. The paths and colourful parterres are interrupted by extravagant fountains. There is also an artificial grotto and fake ruins, once used as a theatre.

Bayreuth is a city with medieval roots, although the architecture of the Margrave Wilhelmine left its elegant baroque imprint. The city is world famous for its astounding *Markgräfliches Opernhaus* (the Margrave's most beautiful gift to the city) and the Wagner Festival, and is scattered with splendid palaces and works of art, which make it one of the most attractive cities in northern Bavaria. The city centre has two castles: the Renaissance-style *Altes Schloss* (sixteenth to seventeenth century) and the sumptuous *Neues Schloss*, which is also touched by the creative hand of the Margrave, but the most representative and romantic castle is located outside the city gates, among wheat fields and woodlands.

The Hermitage was built around the middle of the eighteenth century by the Margrave Georg Wilhelm, as an ascetic refuge from his luxurious court, and was given to Wilhelmine by her husband Friederich, the successor to the throne of Bayreuth.

The Prussian princess was an emancipated, intelligent and energetic woman who was a talented painter, musician and writer. The daughter of Friederich Wilhelm I and favourite sister of Friederich the Great, she could have become the future queen of England, but a mistaken political move by her father took her to Bayreuth, a provincial and colourless city in Franconia. Nevertheless, the young Wilhelmine was not to be outdone, and decided to transform Bayreuth

into a brilliant centre for the arts, using the best artists and artisans of the time. The spartan Hermitage was transformed into a splendid summer residence, in which the Margrave took refuge with her artist friends and penned her memories in emotional writings that became a brilliant piece of literature. The rococo palace became the background for the gardens on which the Margrave focused her creative attention. The gardens of the Hermitage were already famous in Bavaria for their design, which was *avant-garde* for the time.

Inspired by the theatrical effect produced by the position of the gardens, Wilhelmine made changes that satisfied her taste for the *mise-en-scène*. She brought in many statues and artificial ruins, among the most spectacular of which were the ruins of the theatre. Wilhelmine herself and her friend Voltaire appeared on the stage in *Bajazet*, a tragedy by the French playwright Racine.

The *Neues Schloss* confirms the sensation that the buildings are almost a theatrical backdrop for the gardens.

In the centre of the two curved side wings is the isolated *Sonnentempel* (the Sun Temple). Its extravagant covering of fragments of coloured glass and blue and green rocks is absolutely unique. Complementing the dazzling effect are the golden Apollo statues on the cupola of the temple, with a team of four horses pulling the sun coach, symbol of absolute power in the style of Louis XIV.

104 right The Sun Temple, dominated by a gilt coach drawn by four horses, is on the Hermitage's formal side, from which the Orangerie extends in two semicircular wings. The outside walls of the complex are covered with fragments of pebbles and coloured rocks, an unusual technique rarely used for exteriors.

104-105 The Hermitage's Old Castle was built by the Margrave Georg Wilhelm. The four-winged structure was then presented to the Margrave Wilhelmine, who added two side wings and transformed the interior.

105 top The sumptuous yet intimate Japanese Room at the Hermitage has enamel relief work, some of which, the gift of Friederich the Great, comes from the Far East. Other enamel work was based on ideas by the Margrave Wilhelmine and completed with her assistance. This photo shows a detail of the ceiling with its unusual Oriental motifs.

106 top left *The original furnishings still stand in the Gothic style chapel. The lavish altar by Junker, completed in 1614, is one of the most precious pictorial works of the period.*

106 top right *The Bed Chamber is in true Neoclassical style, decorated with panelling and a pink silk canopy embroidered with pure gold thread.*

JOHANNISBURG CASTLE
IN ASCHAFFENBURG

The city of Aschaffenburg stands on the Main River in Spessart, the far western corner of Bavaria.

In contrast to the gentle natural landscape, the city is a row of massive stone facades along the river, the most imposing of which is *Schloss* Johannisburg, a legacy of the immense secular power wielded by the bishop princes of Mainz, who reigned from the tenth to the early nineteenth centuries. Before being appointed archbishop and elector of Mainz, Johann Schweikhard von Kronberg had to swear to restore the ruins of the castle of Aschaffenburg, which had been destroyed by the Margrave of Kulmbach. The Renaissance palace, the archbishop's second residence, was built between 1604 and 1614 on a design by Georg Riedinger. A child of his time, the elector yearned for a *grandeur* that would befit his position as elector of the Holy Roman Empire.

He thus created an imposing red sandstone palace, consisting of four wings with a massive tower at each corner, spending the equivalent of forty-five million marks.

The Johannisburg is one of the most important works of the German Renaissance, as well as one of the largest castles in Germany built at one time based on a single design, and is a grandiose introduction to the architecture of state castles typical of the modern era.

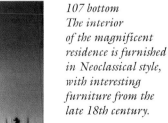

106-107 A witness to the immense secular power of the bishop princes of Mainz, who ruled here from the 10th to the 19th centuries, Johannisburg Castle's imposing facade is reflected in the Main River.

107 top Titus' Arch is depicted in one of the pieces in the collection of little cork models on display at Johannisburg Castle.

107 bottom The interior of the magnificent residence is furnished in Neoclassical style, with interesting furniture from the late 18th century.

SCHLOSS *EHRENBURG*

108 top left
The picture is a view of one of the two side pavilions, with the facade adorned by architectural balconies.

108 top right The main entrance to Ehrenburg opens to form the Court of Honour on the broad square. The three segments that make it up date back to

the late 17th-century baroque structure, but the facade was redone in neo-Gothic English style in the early 19th century.

108-109
The marvelous Party Room, which dates back to the time of Duke Albrecht, is almost entirely covered with extraordinary stucco

decorations by Carlo Domenico and Bartolomeo Lucchese. It is known as the Hall of Giants due to the twenty-eight massive male caryatid figures who appear to hold up the ceiling. Each one holds a candelabra in an outstretched arm, with the other arm bent above his head to support the ceiling.

Coburg is the capital of Coburgerland, located among the hills of upper Franconia and the last remnants of the Thuringian Forest. Its beautiful historic downtown area still exudes that aristocratic elegance that characterized it until the last century. On the broad Schlossplatz, where fine summer concerts are held among the splendid flowerbeds, is *Schloss* Ehrenburg, the ducal palace and residence of the Saxe-Coburg-Gotha family until 1920. The powerful family was allied with royal families all over Europe. Albert, the beloved prince consort of Queen Victoria of England, whose descendants still rule the British throne, was descended from this family. Queen Victoria herself, who was a frequent guest at Ehrenburg, was responsible for introducing something which was at the time an absolute luxury and novelty, and which now, among the astonishing riches of the residence, is one of the most popular curiosities for visitors: Germany's first flush toilet, a convenience to which the queen had become accustomed in England and which she was absolutely unwilling to do without during her long stays at Coburg.

Ehrenburg has a neo-Gothic appearance, primarily due to the final retouches of 1811, but the original edifice was built in 1543 by order of Duke Johann Ernst, on the site of a thirteenth-century convent. At that time he was one of the first rulers north of the Alps to abandon a safer but undeniably more austere fortified dwelling on a hill for a more comfortable, stately residence in the centre of the city. After the Thirty Years' War, during which Coburg was invaded by enemy troops, the castle was abandoned for nearly a half a century. Duke Albrecht occupied it in 1680 and restored and remodelled it according to the baroque tastes of the times. He is responsible for the opulent Hall of Giants, which owes its artistic importance to its masterpiece of stucco decoration. Neoclassicism left a clear mark on Ehrenburg; many rooms were remodelled under Duke Ernst I (1806-1844), and most of the rococo and baroque furniture was replaced by furnishings, bronzes and clocks bought especially in Paris.

The furnishings in the rooms have been left almost completely as they were, including the family photographs of Queen Victoria on the tables, and this is one of the castle's major attractions. In its less stately and more residential rooms, the place almost seems still inhabited, offering a rare glimpse into a usually inaccessible world.

109 The portraits of Coburg nobles in the Family Room include a portrait of Prince Albert, who married his cousin Victoria, the Queen of England. Devastated by the death of her beloved husband at only 42 years old, the queen (who ruled for 54 years) mourned him until her death.

FORTIFIED CASTLES, MEDIEVAL SPLENDOURS

110 top In 1277 Pottenstein Castle, located on a steep cliff of dolomitic rock, provided refuge for Saint Elizabeth, who had fled Thuringia after the death of her husband. By the 18th century the castle had fallen into ruins: a Nuremberg pharmacist finally put a halt to its destruction in 1878 when he rebuilt several parts of the castle.

Bavaria's position in the heart of Europe has made it a territory of transit, sometimes for purposes of trade, but more often for conquest.

Ever since ancient times, primitive fortresses of wood and earth were erected to defend the population. When the Romans conquered the ancient territory of Bavaria, they often built their rock fortresses on the ruins of primitive fortifications which they themselves had vanquished.

As the centuries passed, the realm of Bavaria expanded and became richer and more enticing to the peoples on its borders. The Bavarians themselves felt an increasing sense of independence and a desire for conquest.

All over Europe trade was beginning to flourish, and important trading routes, such as the Salt Road and the Iron Road, were opening up and traversing its borders. Numerous fortresses sprang up to protect cities, rivers and valleys and defend these merchant routes. This type of defensive architecture reached its zenith during the medieval Age of Chivalry.

In mountainous areas, the fortresses are perched on rocky heights in impossible positions, and almost seem sculpted in the rock.

Their position alone was sufficient to dissuade the most hardened assailant. Fortified castles in hilly areas are true fortified citadels, often with various circular fortifications, and from a distance look like giant transatlantic liners floating in a green sea.

110 bottom A visit to the medieval castle of Rosenburg, near Riedenburg on eastern Bavaria's border with Franconia, is a true trip back into the past. In its courtyard, trainers in period costumes and their birds of prey provide visitors with an extraordinary demonstration of hunting with these majestic birds, taking observers back into the past as they watch these raptors gliding over the beautiful Altmühl Valley.

On the plains, in addition to massive walls, the only other defence possible was to surround the castle with water, using the natural attributes of the countryside. Thus, many of the towers and bastions that we still find so romantic today are reflected in lakes, rivers, ponds and wide moats. Wherever they are built, and however diverse their appearances, their structures, all designed for defence, have much in common, including walls, turrets and slit windows to protect their defenders, massive gates with drawbridges, watchtowers, guard towers with alarm bells, wells and granaries to resist sieges, and the residential portion for the noble and his court, a bit more comfortable than the other wings but still very austere and cramped.

The lack of space was another common denominator for these fortresses, which during times of war became refuges for a majority of the population. By the end of the Middle Ages, changing techniques of war made these structures obsolete, and in pursuit of a new-found taste for comfort and luxury, the nobles abandoned them. Many fell into ruin, but many were recovered and restored: the largest have been converted into museums with art galleries open to the public, and the smaller ones were purchased by private parties who restored them not only as residences, but also as lovely inns, comfortable restaurants or small private museums.

110-111 The tall, slender tower of Veldenstein fortress is the emblem of Neuhaus a.d. Pegnitz, an ancient village with red-tiled roofs and typical lattice-work houses. In 1007 this important commercial city on the southern edge of the dense Veldenstein forest was conquered by Heinrich II for his new Bamberg diocese.

111 top The Niederhaus fortress is connected to the Oberhaus fortress above by a long rounds walk which has a splendid view of the city, with the colourful confluence of the three rivers that surround it: the pale Danube, the muddy Inn and the deep green Ilz.

112-113 The gracious little town of Füssen has an imposing castle with turreted walls and portals known as Hohes Schloss, which dates back to a 4th-century Roman fort. The fortress was built in 1219 and underwent many changes over the centuries, but the transformation into a castle for the bishop princes did not alter its defensive character.

114-115 The village of Burghausen with its elegant architecture characteristic of the Inn-Salzach region stands on the banks of the Salzach River under the protective gaze of its massive fortress, which guarded the city's profitable salt trade for over 300 years.

114 top In order to strengthen the defensive power of the fortress, the six courtyards were independent and fortified, separated by deep moats that permitted troops and inhabitants to resist assaults and sieges for long periods of time.

THE BURGHAUSEN FORTRESS

" *T* here is the underground city!" cried Napoleon as he crossed the Salzach River with his troops. It was an appropriate comment, reflecting the defensive position of the city in its role as an important military post along the Austrian-Bavarian border. Featuring the colourful architecture typical of the Inn-Salzach area, this lovely city unwinds along the Salzach River, its main street in the shadow of the longest fortress in Europe, a true citadel 1,030 metres in length.

There are no longer any traces of the old castle from the year 1090, but the foundation walls, the cellars of Duke Henry XII and the inner chapel dating from the thirteenth century can still be admired in the main courtyard.

In the late fifteenth century, the continuous threat of the Turks prompted an expansion of the fortress that went on for more than ten years; today, most of its structures date from 1480 to 1490. In medieval times, each of the six courtyards that comprise it were separated by a moat, a drawbridge and a gate. To the north, the tuff rise on which the fortress was built expands to one hundred metres wide, becoming a low terrace. This was the most vulnerable part of the fortress, and indeed, its largest edifice, which enclosed the sixth courtyard to the north and was used as a granary and barracks, was demolished by Napoleon so that it could never again be used as a defence against him. Shortly thereafter, most of the

structures which stood around what is now a large green square, were sold to private parties. This was the fate of almost all the buildings, which are still occupied by private owners. Although the current owners do not permit their homes to be visited, as you pass from courtyard to courtyard among the still-inhabited buildings within the castle walls, there is an evocative impression that the fortress is still alive, as it was in the past, when the buildings that now are home to the tranquil citizens of Burghausen served as quarters for soldiers, servants, court officials and their families. In the sixth courtyard the names of the buildings still echo the functions of the people that inhabited them: to the west, built in the fourteenth century, are the guest quarters and those of the chancellor and the beneficiaries. The round towers to the east and that of the income registrar, carpenters and chimney sweeps, date back to the fifteenth century, when the buildings, the craftsmen's workshops and a stable completed the courtyard. Crossing a bridge, which is no longer the original, you come to the fifth courtyard. To the east is the building that housed the tax office, and behind it is the courtyard's main point of interest, the outer chapel. This Gothic gem was built by the royal couple that is still commemorated every four years at Landshut, in a famous historical reconstruction of their wedding — Georg the Rich, the Duke of

115 top The chapel is the point of attraction in the fifth courtyard. A jewel of Gothic style with its pointed bell tower, it was donated to the castle by Duke George the Rich and Jadwiga, the daughter of the King of Poland.

115 bottom The early 16th-century clock tower with its added kiosk stands in the centre of the broad green open space in the sixth courtyard.

116 left This wooden
statue of St. Martin
stands in the inner
chapel of the main
courtyard.

116 right
The Ducal Hall in
the first courtyard
holds two museums.
The Civic Museum
contains terracotta
items, antique
furniture, weapons,
uniforms and folk

costumes, while the
State Museum
displays paintings
and tapestries form
the national
Bavarian collection.
The photo shows an
ornamental relief of
the castle.

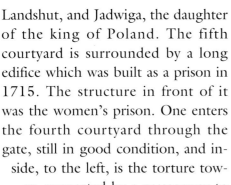

Landshut, and Jadwiga, the daughter of the king of Poland. The fifth courtyard is surrounded by a long edifice which was built as a prison in 1715. The structure in front of it was the women's prison. One enters the fourth courtyard through the gate, still in good condition, and inside, to the left, is the torture tower, connected by a passageway to the Witches' Tower, which was used as a prison. In the courtyard, the present-day youth hostel is located in a building that was built in the nineteenth century on the site of the great granary. To the west is a house with a beautiful Gothic stairway, and before it, somewhat hidden behind the granary, is the former home of the granary custodian, one of the most interesting and unique houses of the fortress.

The third courtyard was the arsenal, the ground floor of which was used as a granary. The walls that surround it have swallowtail battlements, in the Middle Ages known as "sermon fingers." The perfectly preserved Georg Gate is the barrier that protects the two main courtyards, the heart of the fortress. In the second courtyard is the well, the oven, a stable for 100 horses and the servants' and grooms' quarters. Access to the first courtyard is over a moat 8

metres deep and 28 metres wide and two gates. The various parts of the residential castle, which now holds the State Museum and the Municipal Museum, open up around the courtyard, but for centuries the walls served as a defence and sometimes as a prison for the lords of the time. Even the legendary (and unlucky) Jadwiga, the protagonist of the famous *Landshut Marriage*, ended her days there after many years of confinement. The official reason for her imprisonment was that she had borne her husband no male heirs, but the reports of the time maintained that the duchess, ignored by an increasingly absent and unfaithful husband, was caught seeking solace with the fortress' cook.

116-117 This photo shows a view of the complex's oldest buildings, which date back to the Gothic period. In the 1st century BC there was a Celtic fortress on the southernmost point of the ridge (the current position of the residential palace). The fortress took on its present form over the centuries, but the inner chapel and the castle cellars from 1200 can still be admired in their original form.

117 bottom The stairway on the left wing of the first courtyard, Dürnitz, leads to a Renaissance Gothic room with round arches, which served as a meeting and ball room. The ballroom for servants and domestics was on the first floor.

HARBURG CASTLE

118 top left and 119 top One enters the main courtyard through a series of medieval defensive structures. The courtyard is surrounded by a group of interesting functional buildings, including the Kastenhaus, which was once a granary, and the Burgvogtei, a 16th-century castle. The Diebsturm, a 12th-century tower which is the oldest part of the complex, connects to the courtyard.

118 bottom left Seven centuries of history have been written within these walls. The austerely furnished rooms with their old antique furniture are adorned with beautiful caisson ceilings.

118 top right Immersed within the calm countryside, the residential fortress of the counts of Oettingen has gazed down on the tranquil flow of the Wörnitz River for centuries.

118-119 The pale walls of the fortress, with towers and turrets overlooking the forest, stand out against the green landscape.

Near the famous Romantic Road in the northwestern part of Bavarian Allgäu-Swabia, this castle, which seems to come from a fable of dragons and knights, dominates the lovely town with its lattice-work houses. Its towers and turrets rising out of the green woods that surround it make it easy to imagine that its impregnable walls are protecting the long slumber of Sleeping Beauty. First mentioned in an official document in 1093, this fortress was built to defend the imperial road from Nördlingen to Donauwörth. In 1295 the castle was given to the faithful Counts — later Princes — of Oettingen, a privilege which became hereditary in 1407 (their descendants still own it). Today the castle, an architectural hodgepodge that spans seven centuries, is one of the best preserved complexes of its type in southern Germany. The main courtyard can be reached through a series of medieval defensive structures and is surrounded by several interesting functional structures, such as the *Kastenhaus*, the old granary and the *Burgtvogtei*, the sixteenth-century manor house, now transformed into a small, picturesque hotel-restaurant. The oldest part still standing, the *Diebsturm*, or Thieves' Tower, dates back to the twelfth century. The *Fürstenbau*, a sixteenth-century structure, houses the priceless collection of art that the lords of the castle collected over the centuries, including some masterpieces in wood by the inimitable Tilman Riemenschneider.

WILLIBALDSBURG FORTRESS

120 The fortress holds the Jura Museum. This splendid Jurassic museum gives an evocative picture of prehistoric life in this part of Bavaria. It has a large collection of fossils found nearby, including enormous fish (top), and a rare, intact example of Archaeopteryx (bottom), the link between reptiles and birds.

120-121 The defensive and war-like aspects of the Willibaldsburg fortress made it an impregnable bulwark protecting the baroque city of Eichstätt below and the important Altmühl River and commercial route. At its peak, the fortress was one of the most sumptuous castles in Germany.

The city of Eichstädt is a small baroque jewel located in the heart of the natural park of the Altmühltal, a valley traversed by the Altmühl River, full of breathtaking scenery and priceless architectural treasures. Above the city stands one of the most important fortified castles in the entire valley. Built on a steep slope for defensive purposes, the large complex with its angular towers was built by order of Bishop Berthold von Eichstätt in 1393 and remained a bishop's residence until 1780. In 1609, the famous architect Elias Holl, who designed the Augsburg City Hall, was hired to build the imposing *Gemmingenbau*. The residential palace now holds the Jura-Museum, with one of the most interesting fossil collections in Bavaria, including unique, extremely rare examples of *Archaeopteryx* found in the area. Willibaldsburg was once one of the most sumptuous castles in Germany. After the Thirty Years' War it was further fortified and transformed into a citadel. Like most fortified residences, with the advent of more peaceful times and government well-being, the bishop princes of Eichstätt decided to build a sumptuous palace in the city, thus giving it the prestigious Residenz with its remarkable rococo and neoclassical rooms.

121 top Magnificent Willibaldsburg emerges in the distance against the placid landscape of the Altmühl Valley.

The English missionary monk Willibald founded Eichstätt in 745 and became its first bishop.

PRUNN CASTLE

122 top left The simple little chapel is embellished by stucco work on the ceiling and a graceful wooden altar.

122 top right The interior of the fortress is quite bare, due in part to the fact that one of its last uses

was as a Franciscan monastery but the decorations around the doors are worthy of interest and the windows offer a bird's eye view of the valley and the river.

122-123 Looking like a continuation of the rock on which

they were built, the walls of the Prunn fortress hid the first manuscript of the Legend of the Nibelungen for two centuries. The manuscript was discovered accidentally during remodelling work in 1575.

The castle can be seen in the distance from the valley.

In seeming defiance of human reason, it was constructed on a rock 70 metres high overlooking the Altmühl River, and appears to be practically suspended from it.

It is impossible not to marvel at how, almost a thousand years ago, such solid and beautiful buildings capable of resisting wartime attacks and the ravages of time could be built in such seemingly impossible positions. While its view from the bottom of the valley is certainly beautiful, the panorama visible from the castle's rooms and walls is truly breathtaking, with a bird's eye view of the Altmühl valley. It runs uninterrupted for kilometres and kilometres, following the tranquil course of the river, which curls through the deep green pine woods, the golden yellow rape fields and the white villages dotted with red. Period documents show that the castle was already in existence in 1037. Its long history has seen many lords, including the von Prunn family, who gave it its name, the Dukes of Bavaria, the brotherhood of the Jesuits of Ingolstadt, and finally, in 1803, the State of Bavaria. The castle is famous for its *Prunn Codex*, an antique manuscript from around 1300, which was accidentally found during a Renaissance restoration of its interior.

The manuscript recounts the first "Song of the Nibelungen," which inspired Wagner to write his Ring cycle.

123 top Since 1037, when the fortress on the promontory was first mentioned, many lords have contended for its possession, including the von Prunn nobles, who gave it its name.

123 bottom The beautiful fortified structure stands precariously on a 70-metre cliff. In ancient times the most formidable fortress in the Altmühl Valley, today it is a perfectly preserved example of a medieval fortress.

THE FORTRESS OF NUREMBERG

Nuremberg is the second largest city in Bavaria and the capital of one of its regions, Franconia. Because of its key position on many important trading routes, the city reached its economic apex in the Middle Ages, and in 1356, in an edict known as the "Golden Bull", the emperor Charles IV ruled that each newly elected German king had to hold his first diet at Nuremberg. With the discovery of America, the economic power of the city declined, but in the seventeenth century Nuremberg was equally famous for its paintings and its sculptures. Its nearly legendary status in the eyes of many Germans continued over time, so that even Hitler chose it as the seat of his government and the future capital of his empire. After the war, the Allies also recognized its symbolic importance and chose it as the seat for the famous Nuremberg trials of surviving Nazi leaders.

The *Burg* (fortress), perched on a rock at the edge of the old city, gives Nuremberg its unmistakable profile. The odd-looking group of buildings that make it up has grown over the centuries and actually consists of two castles joined together. On the eastern tip of the rocky spur is *Burggrafenburg* (the Count's Fortress), which came into the possession of the Zoller family in the twelfth century. This powerful family was at variance with the Imperial City of Nuremberg, which held Kaiserburg, the other fortress on the rock. The conflict went on interminably, and the harshest affront to Count Zoller occurred when the citizens built a new fortified tower (*Luginslandturm*) right in front of his fortress. The tower, completed in only five months while the Count was away travelling, was used to spy on Burggrafenburg. In 1427 the Zoller family lost interest in the old ruin and sold it to the city.

Kaiserburg (the Imperial Fortress), located on the western tip of the promontory, is the most impressive part of the complex. The first fortress was built in 1050 by King Henry III; around the middle of the twelfth century the emperor Conrad III built *Kaiserburg*, which was then expanded

124-125 The city of Nuremberg is first mentioned as "Nuremberc" in an imperial document of 1050. In 1219 it was granted the status of a free imperial city, which it maintained until 1806. Many Imperial Diets were held here, and it was also the seat of the Imperial Court.

125 top A 1492 illustration shows the city surrounded by walls (almost all of which still remain) and dominated by the fortress. The tall towers of the churches of St. Sebald and St. Lawrence can be seen below it; even today they are important artistic monuments in the city.

126 The double Romanesque chapel from the 12th century is architecturally the most important part of the fortress. The large sandstone columns of the lower chapel stand in sharp contrast to the slender columns in the Emperor's Chapel, with vaults which almost seem weightless.

and transformed into an imperial residence by Frederick I Barbarossa around 1200. The German empire had no capital, and its emperors and their entourages moved from one residence to another. It is easy to imagine the importance of the fortress of Nuremberg if you consider that from 1050 to 1571 all emperors stayed there, although none of them for long periods of time. This explains the fact that inside the fortress everything appears quite bare and stripped of furnishings. This is not due to the

fires and wars the fortress suffered, but was how it looked when the Emperor and his court were not there. Indeed, the shrewd, thrifty citizens of Nuremberg loaned their finest furniture and furnishings to the fortress when the Emperor announced a visit. After he left, the owners took everything back home.

The inner courtyard of *Kaiserburg* is enclosed within a long Gothic-style *Palas* with the residential and state rooms of the Emperor and his court. Inside is a lovely two-storey chapel, with the upper floor reserved to the nobility and the lower to the servants. In the centre of the courtyard outside *Kaiserburg*, dominated by the massive Sinwell Tower, is the house that contains the *Tiefer Brunnen* (Deep Well), fully 50 metres deep, which provided water to the fortress as early as the 12th century.

In 1427 the western tip of the promontory was also taken by the city and incorporated into its defences, but it remained the property of the Holy Roman Empire.

The oldest part of the fortress is the *Fünfeckturm* (Pentagonal Tower), the only remaining part of the original fortress, which shares the eastern part of the promontory with the massive *Luginslandturm*. After the Zoller family was driven out, the citizens connected the two towers with the Gothic *Kaiserstallung* (the Imperial Stables), which was then used as a granary and now serves as a youth hostel.

126-127 This is a view of the Tiergärtnertor square at the foot of the Kaiserburg Residential Palace. The home of Albrecht Dürer, now a museum, stands on the square.

127 top The photo shows Kaiserburg's outer court with the Well House in the centre. The Deep Well was dug into the rock to a depth of 50 metres. Two truss structures from the 15th and 16th centuries stand in the southwest corner. The lower part of imposing Sinwell Tower dates back to the 12th century, while the upper portion is from 1560.

THE MARIENBERG FORTRESS

The fortress stands on a hill that dominates the city of Würzburg and the Main River, on the same site where the Celts built their fortifications around 1000 BC. The *Marienkirche* (which can be seen within the fortress), one of the oldest churches in Germany, was built in the eighth century, and in the thirteenth century the construction and fortification of the Marienberg citadel began. From 1253 to 1720 it served as the residence of the bishop princes. The castle was transformed into a citadel through various important construction works, which were completed by bishop Rudolf von Scherenberg (1466-1495). Its present-day appearance is the work of bishop Julius Echter von Mespelbrunn (1573-1617). The Mainfrankisches Museum, Franconia's art museum, is located in the Arsenal. It holds a superb collection of wooden sculptures by one of Germany's greatest sculptors of wood, Tilman Riemenschncider. Riemenschneider lived in Würzburg from 1483 to 1531, when he was killed in a bloody battle during the Peasants' Revolt. At the entrance to the museum is an interesting portrait gallery with portraits of the electors of Würzburg, including the man responsible for building the Residenz, Johann Philipp von Schönborn.

128 top
The surrounding moat has been transformed into pleasant gardens where summer shows are held. In the background, one can glimpse the baroque, onion-shaped cupola of the Kiliani Tower, built when the castle was being fortified in the 13th century.

128 centre The Main and Franconia Museum located in the former arsenal and bastion of Echter offers a representative look at 2,000 years of regional history. Its works are significant and varied, including items such as swords and weapons from this arsenal, famous paintings by local artists and forest rangers, sculptures by Tilman Riemenschneider, handicrafts and everyday objects and old folk costumes.

128 bottom The great winepresses in the arsenal's old section tell the story of wine-growing in the area.

128-129 Resting on a hill covered with vineyards, the Marienberg fortress, an important work of defensive architecture, dominates the city of Würzburg and the Main River.

129 top
The Romanesque
Marienkirche *is the
oldest monument
in Marienberg.
It was built on the
hill in the 7th
century as a sign
of devotion to the
Virgin Mary, and
the fortress was later
built around it.*

130 top left
This photo clearly shows the defensive power of the fortress. One of the two circles of walls with its massive guard towers can be seen below the Veste Coburg's high, sheer walls.

130 top right
The Veste Coburg is one of the largest fortresses in Germany. Its imposing oval form, 200 metres by 80 in size, gave it the name of Fränkische Krone, the crown of Franconia.

VESTE COBURG

130-131 *One enters from the east side over an 18th-century bridge through a baroque portal from 1671. The door to the back, which leads to the first circle of walls, is surmounted by a tower built in 1911 by the czar Ferdinand of Bulgaria, from the house of Coburg-Gotha.*

131 top
The Fürstenbau, *the princely palace built in the 16th century, faces the inner courtyard. Today's facade is the result of remodelling in the lattice-work style of Franconia.*

131 bottom *The thick barrier of the second wall is the last defensive bastion and completely surrounds the inner courtyards, where there are various residential and utility buildings.*

One of the most beautiful fortresses in Europe, Veste Coburg stands on the top of a hill occupied by the Ehrenburg, the city palace park, which reaches the outermost of its three circular fortifications.

From a distance, the numerous watchtowers and the gabled roofs rise from the bands of walls like the points of a crown, giving this fortress its Bavarian name of *Fränkische Krone*, or the Crown of Franconia. The city of Coburg, located in the far north of Franconia, was under the jurisdiction of the Dukes of Saxe-Coburg-Gotha until 1920, when the citizens voted to join Upper Franconia, thus becoming Bavarian. The fortress boasts 750 years of history. In 1353 it belonged to the Wettin family, the rulers of Saxony and Thuringia, and in the sixteenth century it became one of their main residences.

The descendants of the Wettin family, the Dukes of Coburg, used it as a residence until 1918. The Gothic-style oldest portion was built between the fourteenth and sixteenth centuries, when the first circle of fortifications was constructed.

During the sixteenth century the fortress was transformed into a citadel, and Lucas Cranach the Elder, who stayed there often, helped transform it into a princely residence.

The outer bastions were added during the following two centuries.

The *Steinerne Kemenate*, which

holds a rich collection of art, with works by Cranach, Dürer, Schongauer and Rembrandt, is located to the left of the beautiful courtyard.

In the Hunting Room, the 1632 wall covering, with rare inlay work and carvings, is one of the most beautiful works of its kind.

In 1530 Martin Luther took refuge within its walls, where he paced the silent gardens and rooms as the Diet of Augsburg deliberated its verdict in his heresy trial. The great reformer's room in the fortress can still be visited today.

132 In the early
1500's, Lucas
Cranach the Elder
often stayed at the
fortress. This photo
shows one of his
paintings at the Veste
Coburg, a portrait
of Johann der
Beständige, the bishop
prince of Saxony.

132-133 The interior
of the Prince's Palace
is richly furnished
with Renaissance
and baroque
furniture.

133 top One of the
most important
rooms in the fortress
is the Luther Room,
named after Martin
Luther, who stopped
at the Veste Coburg
in 1530. A famous
portrait of the
reformer by Lucas
Cranach the Elder
hangs on one of the
walls.

133 centre
A collection of coaches
and sleds is on display
on the ground floor of
the Herzoginbau.
Of special note are
the wedding coaches
from the 16th century
and the tournament
sleds from the 17th to
the 18th centuries.

133 bottom A lavish
collection of weapons
and war apparatus
can be seen in the
Guard Room.

136 As a palace
within a park,
Nymphenburg is
quite different from
other compact palaces
like Versailles.
The entire facade
is designed to provide
access to the park: the
galleries that connect
the two side wings
open onto the
gardens, and even the
old central portion on
the ground floor has
wide passageways
through which coaches
once passed.

INDEX

ILLUSTRATION CREDITS